Hawaiian Word Book

Illustrated by
Robin Yoko Burningham

with Foreword by
Lokomaika'iokalani Snakenberg

The Bess Press
P.O. Box 22388
Honolulu, HI 96822

Executive Editor: Ann Rayson
Design & Typography: Richard Wirtz

Library of Congress

CATALOG CARD NO.: 82-73895

Burningham, Robin Yoko
    Hawaiian Word Book
Honolulu, Hawaii: Bess Press
100 pages   illustrations, glossary-Hawaiian English, English Hawaiian

TABLE OF CONTENTS

FOREWORD

Teachers and parents have often commented about the lack of good quality and attractive materials that deal with the study of Hawaiian language and culture. Often we see books in the stores which are very tourist-oriented with no true appreciation of the depth and complexity of our Hawaiian heritage. Hawaiian words are often used incorrectly and frequently spelled wrong.

This *Hawaiian Word Book* is a serious attempt by the Bess Press to make available, at an inexpensive price, a book for our youth and older people alike who have an interest in learning the basic vocabulary of the *'ōlelo makuahine* (mother tongue) of this *'āina* (land).

The words which are illustrated so beautifully by Robin Yoko Burningham are basic vocabulary dealing with various aspects of Hawaiian culture. They come from such areas as the *'ohana* (family), social life and relations, nature, Hawaiian lifestyle, food, body parts and clothing along with basic verbs and adjectives used in the language.

The lists from which these basic words were drawn represent efforts over a year's period by two colleagues and myself to group together Hawaiian vocabulary from very basic and culturally important terms to more general ones identifying ancient and modern Hawaiian and imported values, practices, objects and people. The lists were compiled by Dr. Emily 'Ioli'i Hawkins (Assistant Professor of Hawaiian Language, University of Hawai'i-Mānoa), Haunani Bernardino (Hawaiian Language Coordinator, Queen Lili'uokalani Children's Center), and myself after long hours of discussions and consultations with *kūpuna* and other Hawaiian language instructors.

The vocabulary in this book is for all elementary learners of the Hawaiian language whether they be children in our elementary schools or students in high schools, colleges or adult courses. Enjoy the illustrations and *holomua i ke a'o 'ana i ka 'ōlelo Hawai'i* (make progress in your study of the Hawaiian language).

Robert M. Lokomaika'iokalani Snakenberg
Hawaiian language instructor

Social Life
and
Relations

aliʻi	kāne	makua
hoahānau	keiki (kama)	mākua
inoa	keiki kāne	makua kāne
kahuna	kupuna	makua kāne hanauna
kāhuna	kūpuna	makuahine
kaikamahine	kupuna kāne	makuahine hanauna
kamaiki	kupuna wahine	ʻohana
kanaka	kupunahine	wahine
kānaka	makaʻāinana	wāhine

ALI'I

KAHUNA

MAKA'AINANA

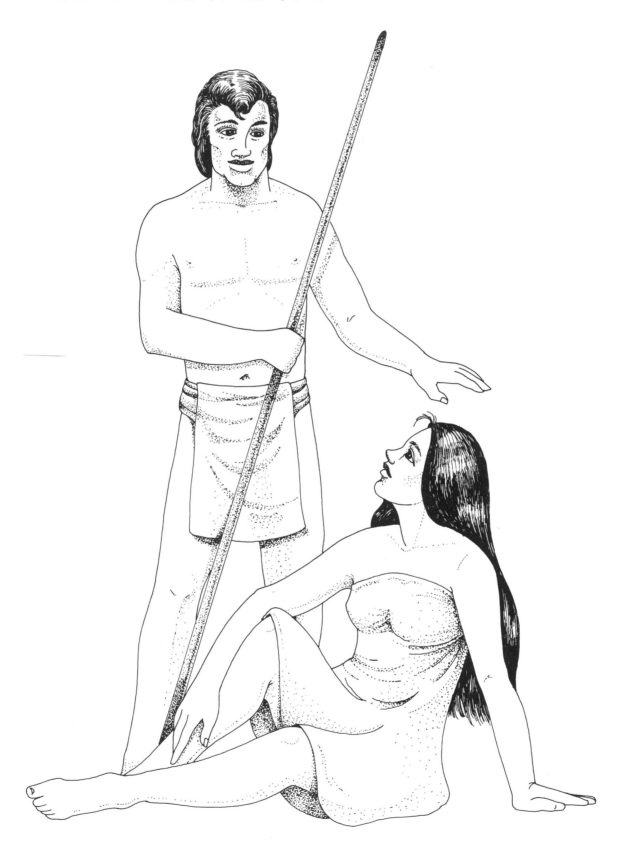

KAUĀ (KAUWĀ)

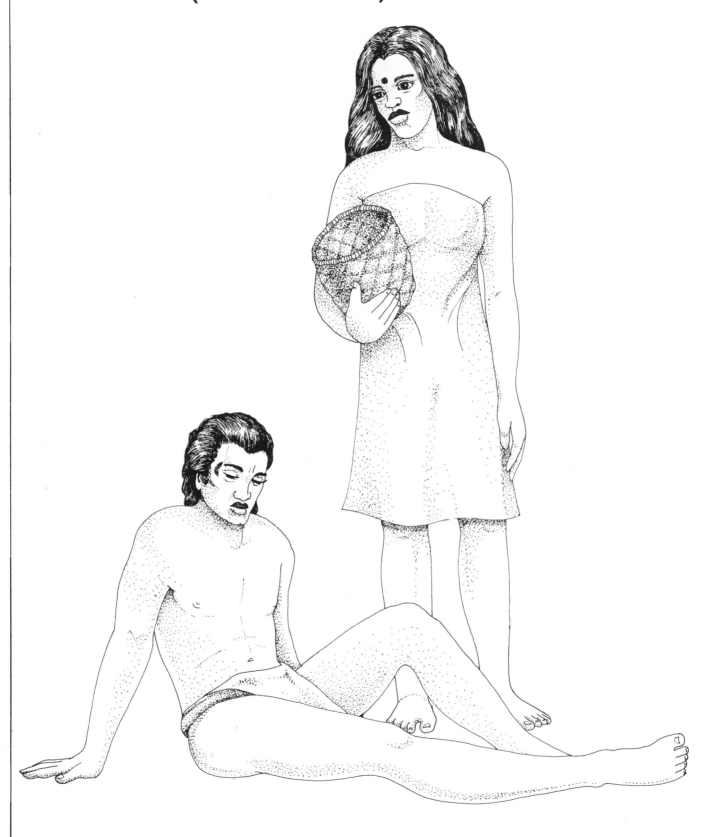

KĀNE

male man

KĀNE

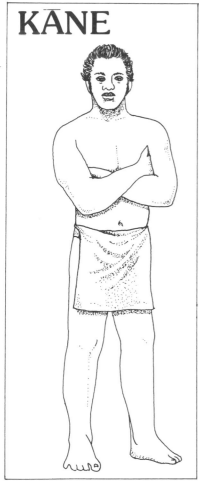

WAHINE

WĀHINE

6

women

KANAKA

KĀNAKA

KEIKI (KAMA)

KAIKAMAHINE

KEIKI KĀNE

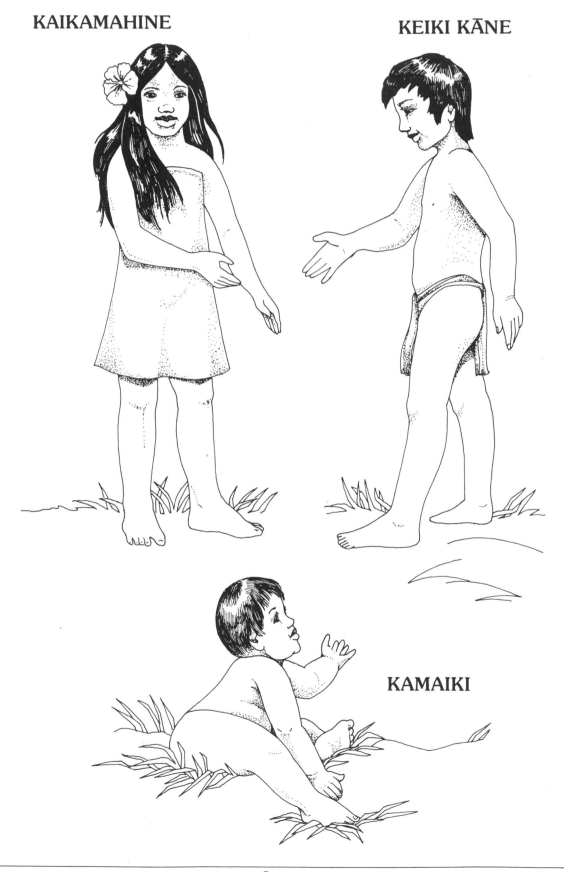

KAMAIKI

MAKUA

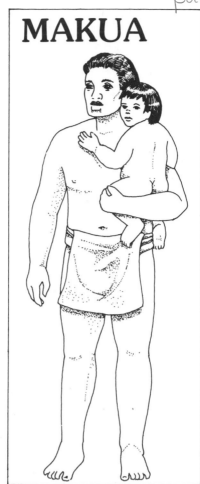

MĀKUA

MAKUA KĀNE
HANAUNA

MAKUA KĀNE

MAKUAHINE

MAKUAHINE
HANAUNA

HOAHANAU

KUPUNA

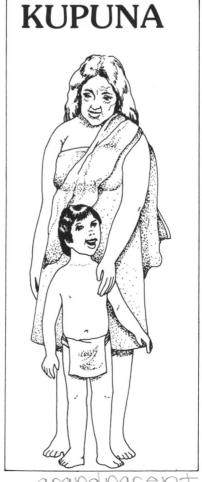

KŪPUNA

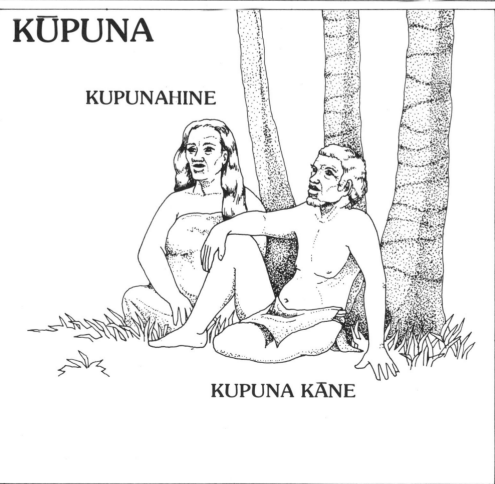

KUPUNAHINE

KUPUNA KĀNE

'OHANA  family

KUPUNA KĀNE

KUPUNAWAHINE

MAKUA KĀNE HANAUNA
(uncle)

MAKUAHINE

KEIKI KĀNE

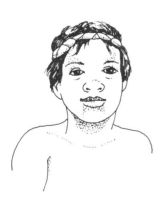

KAIKAMAHINE

KUPUNA KĀNE

KUPUNAWAHINE

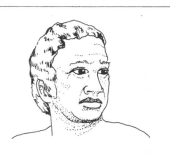

MAKUA KĀNE

MAKUAHINE
HANAUNA

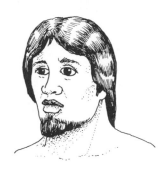

KAMAIKI

KAIKAMAHINE

'OHANA

Hawaiian Lifestyle

akua   lei
aloha   mahalo
ao   moana
hoe   papa heʻenalu
hula   waʻa
kiʻi

13

god

AKUA

image or
KI'I

14

AO

canoe
WA'A

ocean
MOANA

HOE
paddle

16

surfing
PAPA HEʻENALU

flat or level   octopus   wave

HULA

The Body

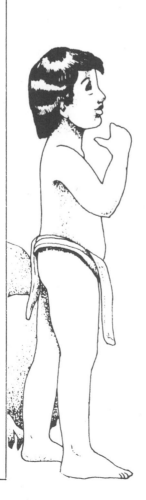

ʻāʻī	lauoho	piko
ake	lima	poʻo
ʻauwae	maka	poʻohiwi
ihu	manamana lima	puʻuwai
iwi	manamana wāwae	ʻūhā
kīkala	naʻau	umauma
kino	ʻōpū	waha
kua	pepeiao	wāwae
kuli		

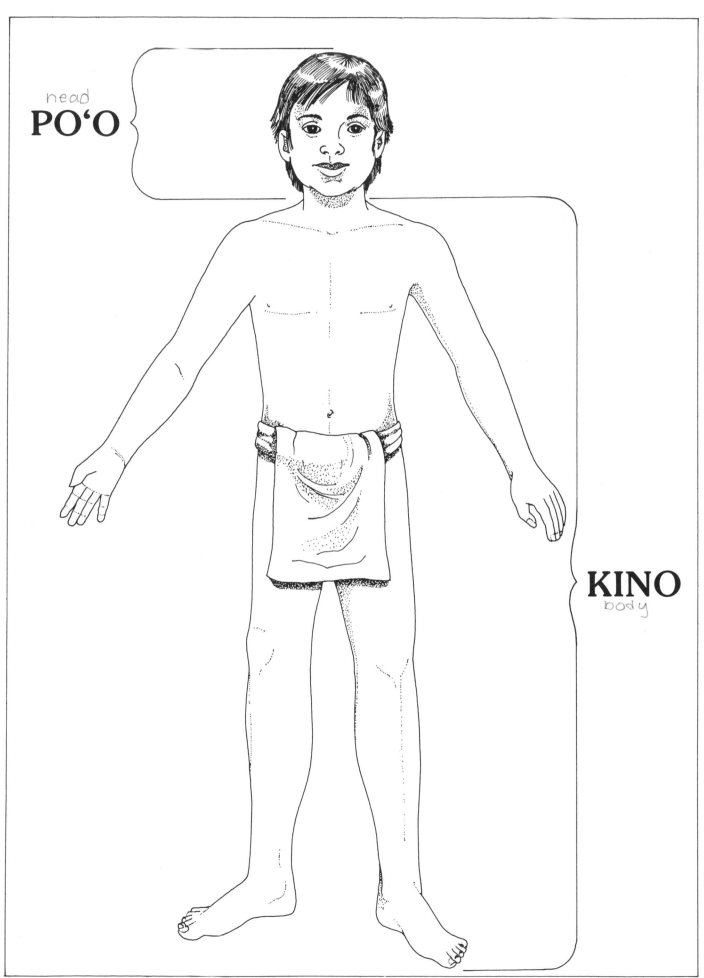

head
PO'O

KINO
body

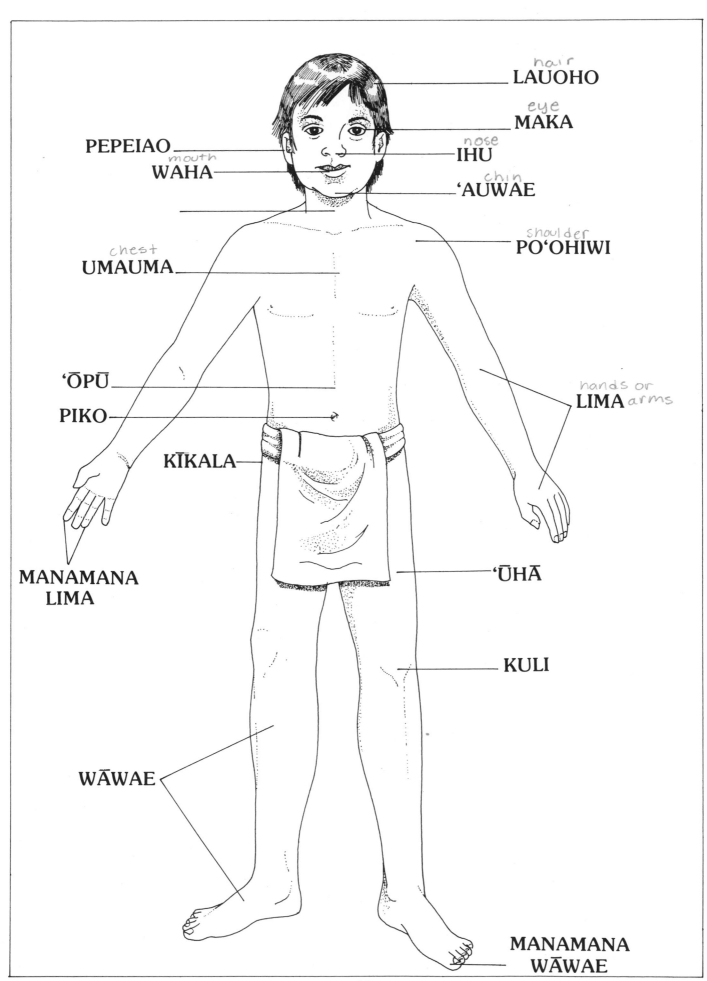

LAUOHO *hair*

MAKA *eye*

PEPEIAO

WAHA *mouth*

IHU *nose*

'AUWAE *chin*

PO'OHIWI *shoulder*

UMAUMA *chest*

LIMA *hands or arms*

'ŌPŪ

PIKO

KĪKALA

MANAMANA LIMA

'ŪHĀ

KULI

WĀWAE

MANAMANA WĀWAE

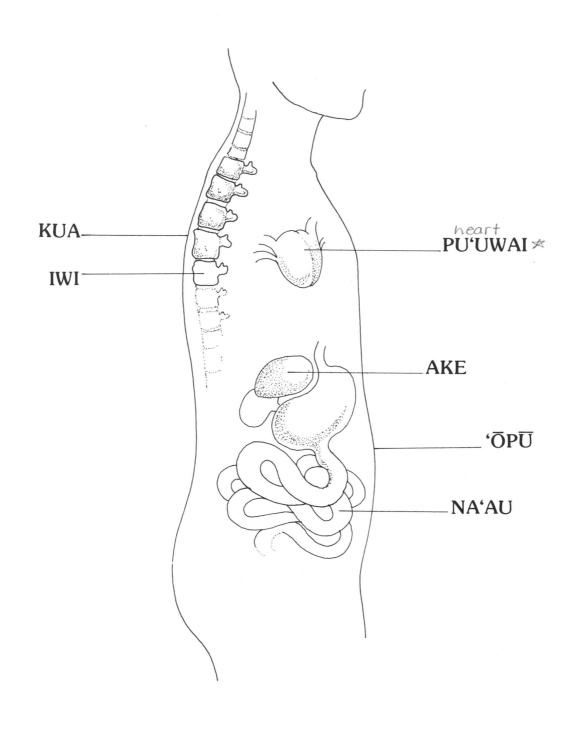

KUA

IWI

heart
PU'UWAI ✷

AKE

'ŌPŪ

NA'AU

MEA'AI
Food

'ai
halakahiki
he'ī
i'a
'īlio
inu
kalo

kō
liliko'i
limu
mai'a
moa
niu
'ono

pa'i'ai
poi
pua'a
'uala
'ulu

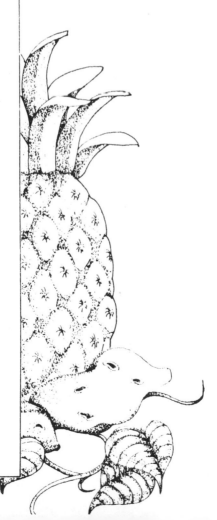

KALO taro

PA'I'AI

POI

✷'UALA
sweet potato

✷HĒ'I
papia

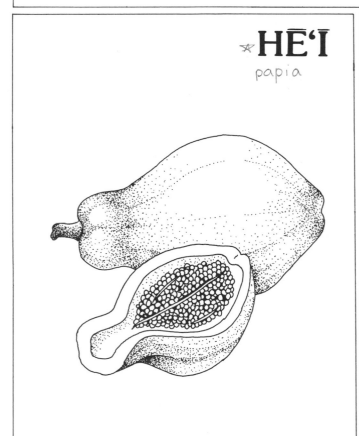

✷MAI'A
bananas

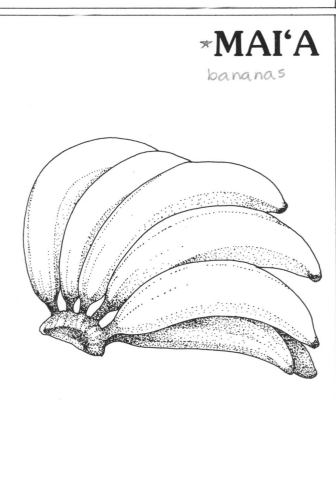

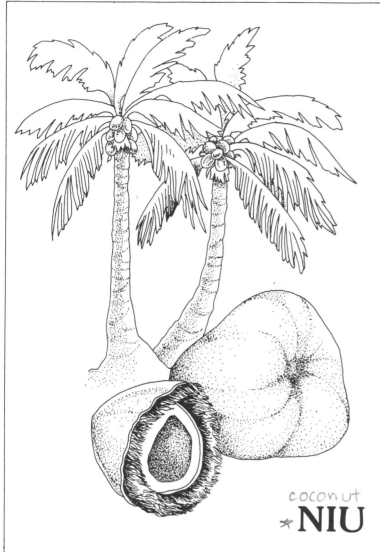

coconut
★ **NIU**

LIMU
seewead

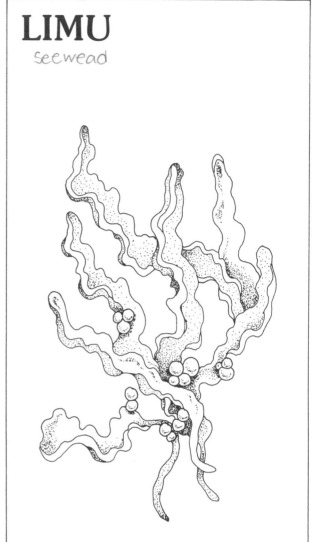

bread fruit
★ **'ULU**

26

HALAKAHIKI

thorney leaves

foreign

Tahiti

pineapple

sugar cane

KŌ ✩

LILIKO‘I

passion fruit

pig
PUA'A

I'A
fish

ʻĪLIO dog

MOA chicken

INU drink

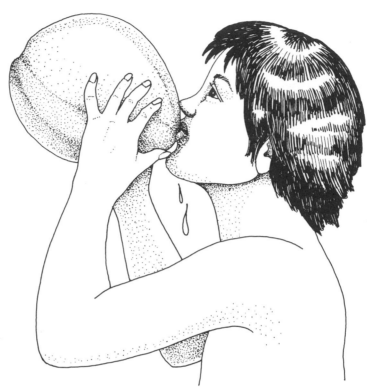

'AI eat

delicious
'ONO

Nature

ahi
ahiahi
ala
ānuenue
'auinalā
awakea
hōkū
kahakai
kai
kakahiaka
kuahiwi

kumulā'au
lā
lā'au
lau
lepo
mahina
makani
manu
mauna
nalu

one
pali
pele
pō
pōhaku
pua
pūpū
ua
wai
wailele

KAKAHIAKA *morning*

AWAKEA *midday*

'AUINALĀ *afternoon*

AHIAHI *evening*

32

LĀ

LĀ or day
sun

PŌ
night

star
HŌKŪ

moon
MAHINA

33

ĀNUENUE
rainbow

UA
rain or *mist*

MAKANI
wind

road
ALA
or path

dirt
LEPO

NALU

wave

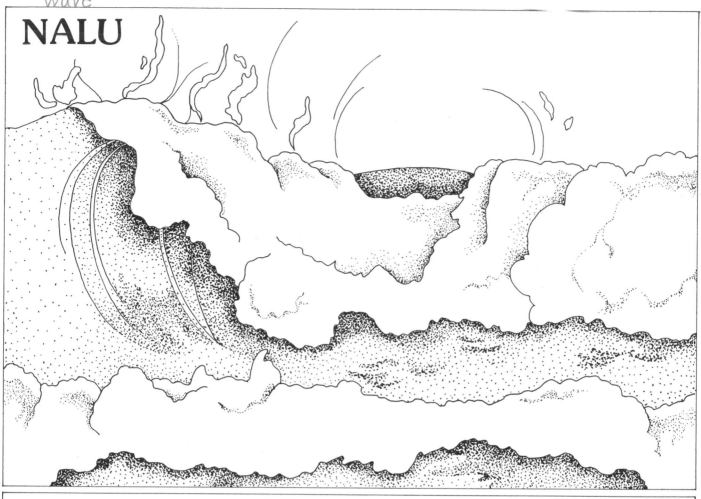

PŪPŪ

shell

KAI sea

sand
ONE

beach
KAHAKAI

LAU

leaf

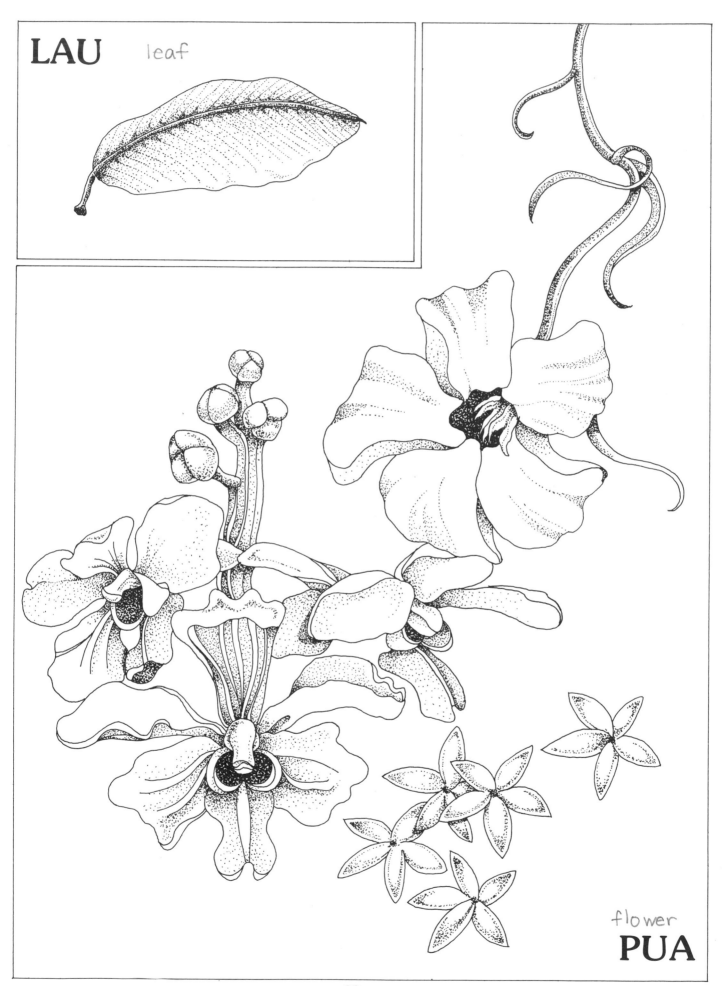

flower

PUA

LĀ‘AU

tree
KUMU LĀ‘AU

wilderness mountains
KUAHIWI

water falls
WAILELE

40

mountain

MAUNA

WAI
water

PŌHAKU
rock

41

cliff
PALI

MANU
bird

AHI *fire*

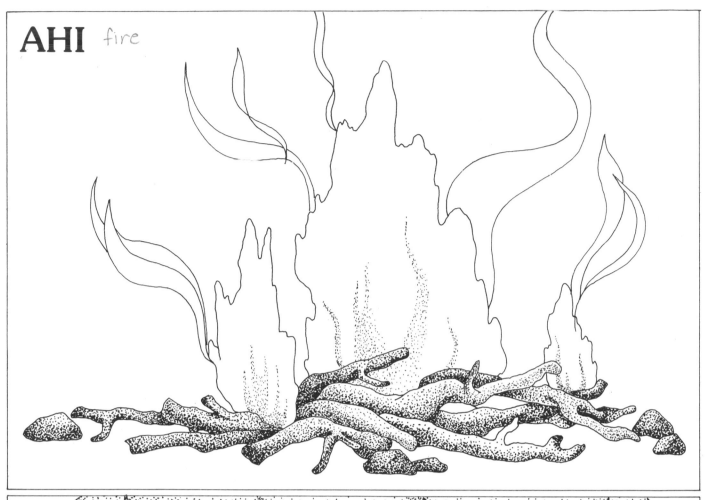

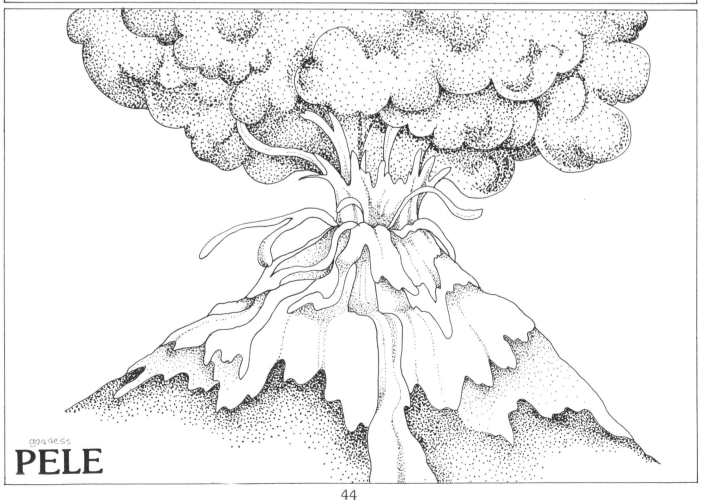

PELE

goddess

44

HALE
House

hale
moena
noho
puka
uluna

house
HALE

ULUNA pillow

MOENA mat

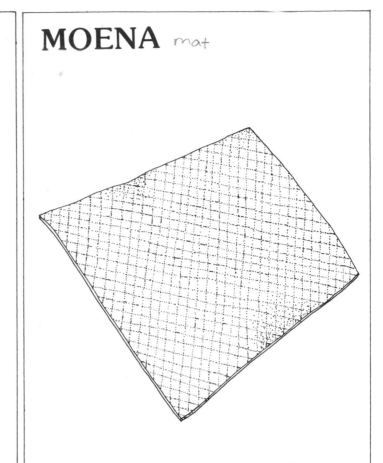

NOHO chair, sit on

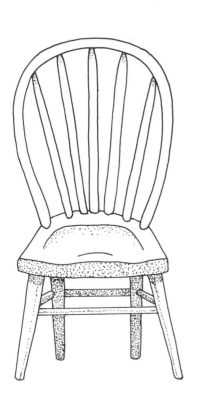

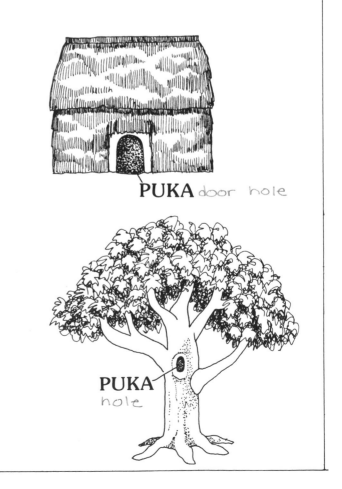

PUKA door hole

PUKA hole

48

HAʻINA
Verbs

ʻauʻau	hiamoe	lohe
haʻawi	holo	moe
hana	hoʻolohe	nānā
hele aku	ʻike	noho
hele mai	kū	ʻōlelo
helu	lele	

HA‘AWI

HANA work or do

51

HELE MAI come toward the speaker

HELE AKU go away

KŪ stand

MOE
ly down

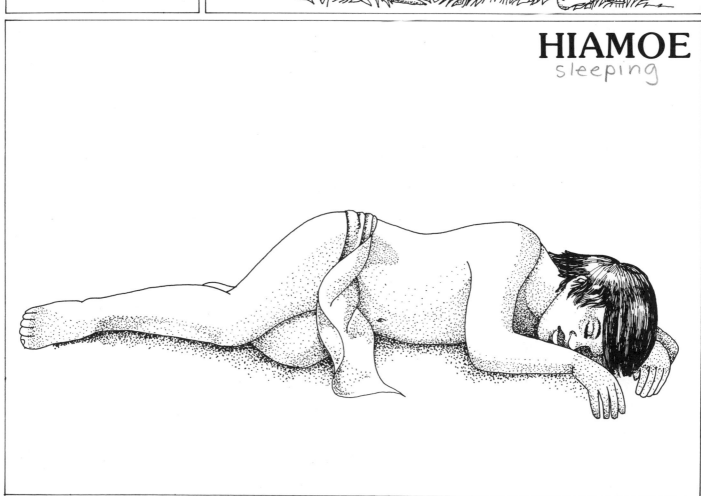

HIAMOE
sleeping

53

HOLO run

LELE leap

NOHO
to sit

'AU'AU
swim

bathing

HOʻOLOHE listen

LOHE hear

56

NĀNĀ

'IKE
think

'ŌLELO speak

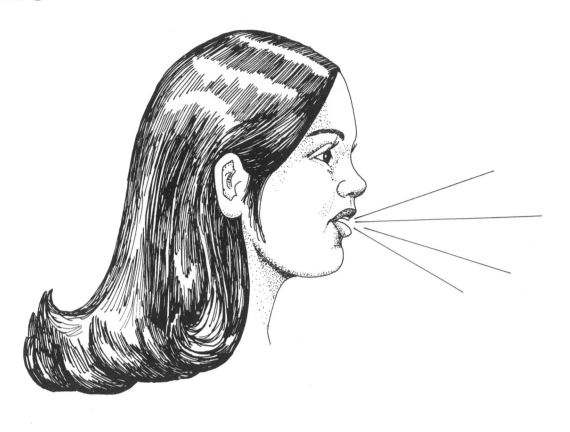

HELU count

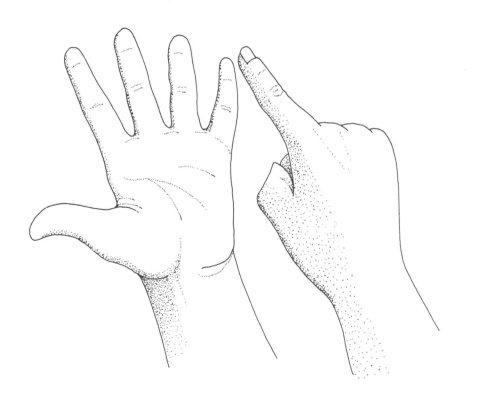

WHERE?
Relative Locations

hope
lalo
loko
luna
ma kai

ma uka
mua
waena
waho

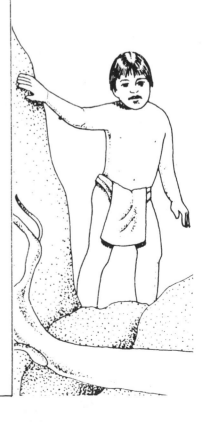

back
HOPE

WAENA
middle

61

LUNA
above

LALO
under

LOKO *inside*

WAHO *outside*

toward mountain

MA UKA

toward the sea

MA KAI

Adjectives

anuanu	kokoke	nui
hau'oli	li'ili'i	pōkole
'ino	lō'ihi	u'i
hou	mālie	'u'uku
kahiko	nani	wela
kaumaha		wīwī

WĪWĪ skinny

MOMONA fat or sweet

NANI
beautiful

U'I
handsome
beautiful

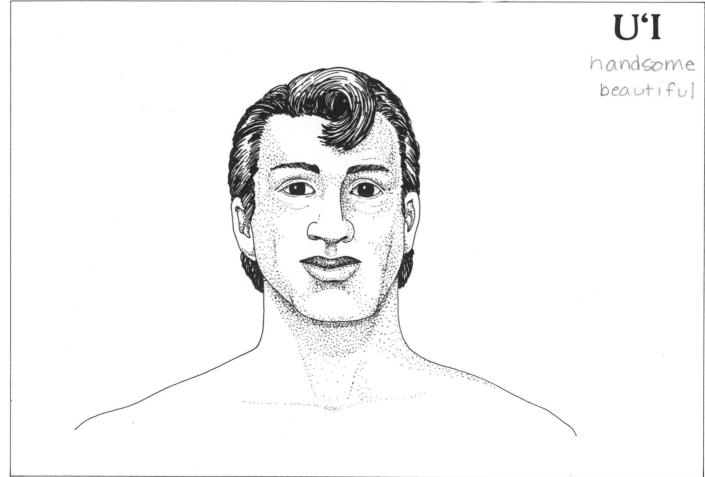

HAU'OLI happy

KAUMAHA sad

WELA
hot

ANUANU
cold

LŌʻIHI

PŌKOLE

70

HOU new

KAHIKO old

NUI
large

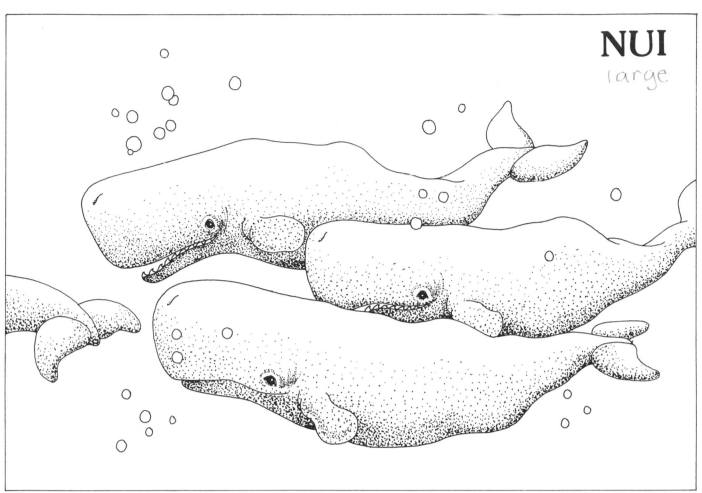

LI'ILI'I

'U'UKU
small

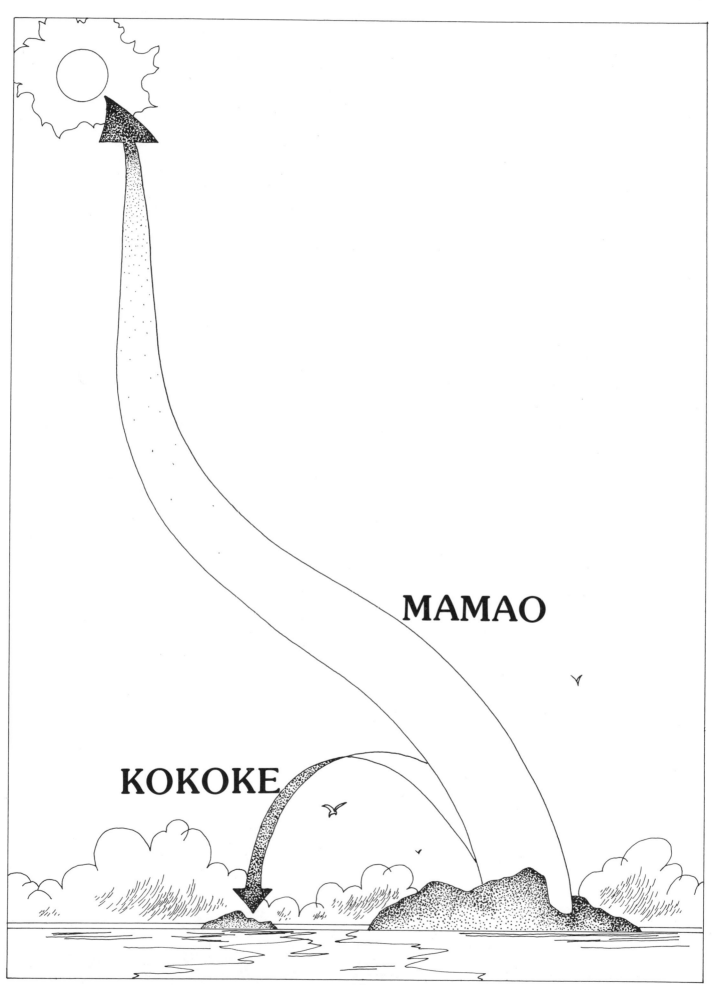

MAMAO

KOKOKE

MĀLIE

ʻINO

74

LOLE
Clothing

kāmaʻa
malo
muʻumuʻu
pāpale
pāʻū

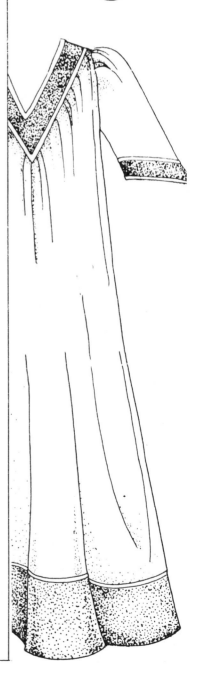

PĀPALE

KĀMAʻA

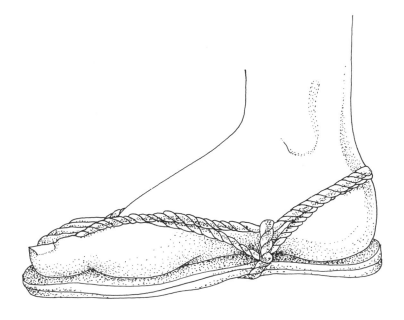

PĀ'Ū

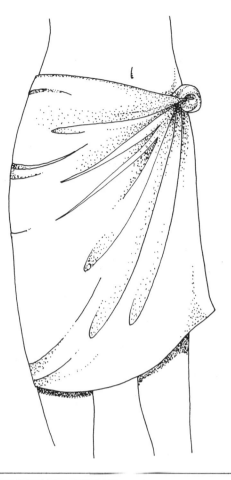

MALO

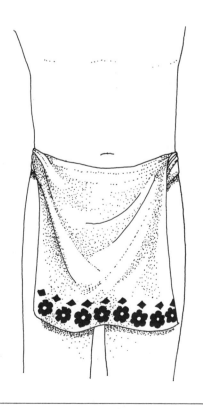

MU'UMU'U

Numbers

'ekahi   'ehiku   'ole
'elua   'ewalu   iwakālua
'ekolu   'eiwa   kanakolu
'ehā   'umi   hanele
'elima   'umikūmākahi   kaukani
'eono   'umikūmālua

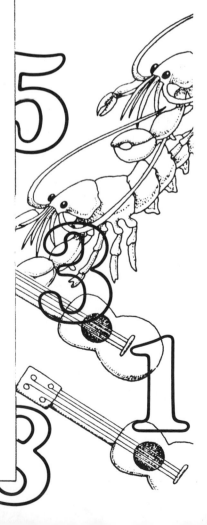

ʻEKAHI   1

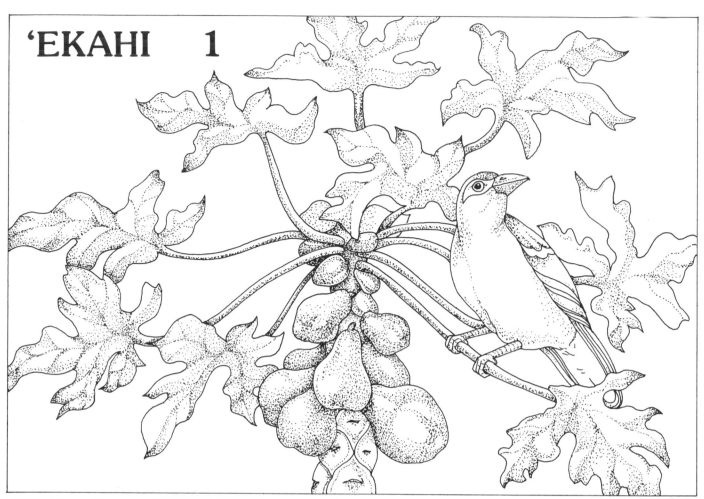

ʻELUA   2

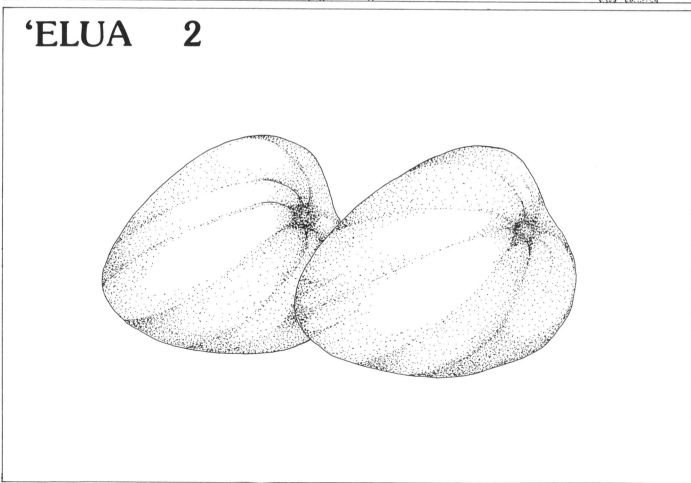

'EKOLU 3

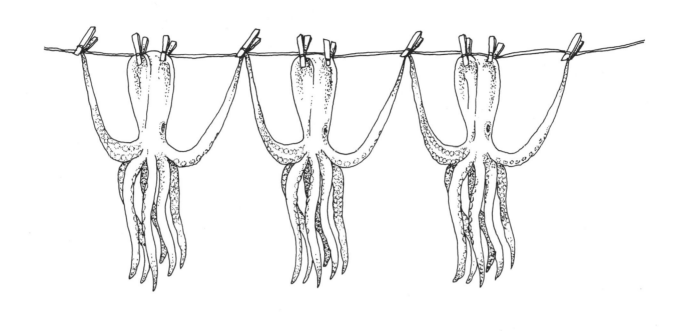

'EHĀ 4

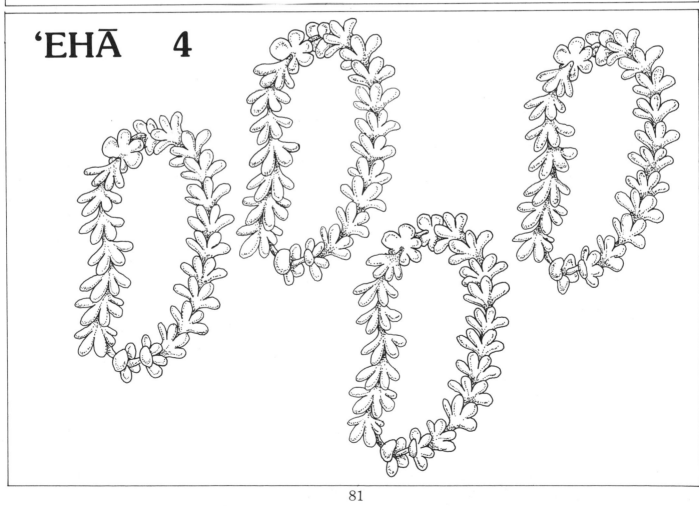

'ELIMA   5

'EONO   6

ʻEHIKU 7

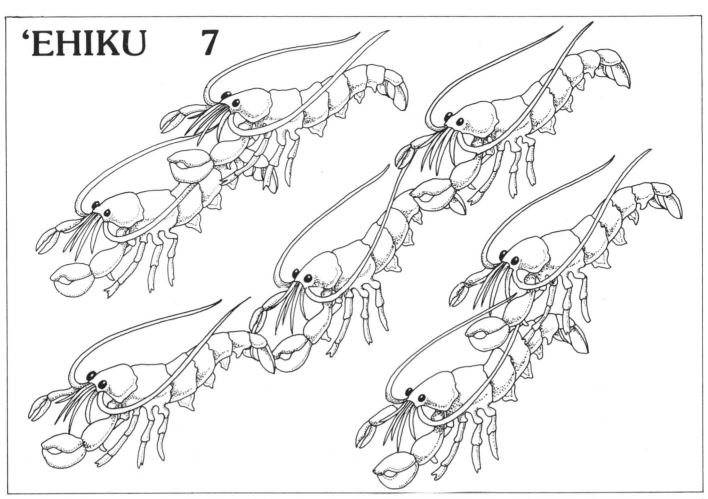

ʻEWALU 8

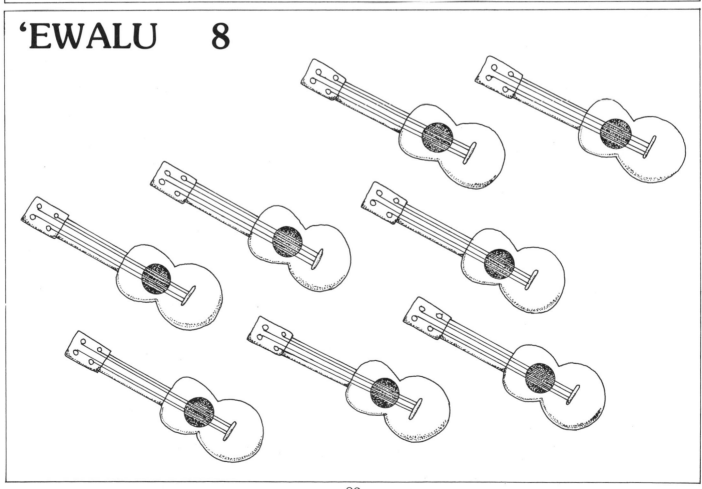

'EIWA   9

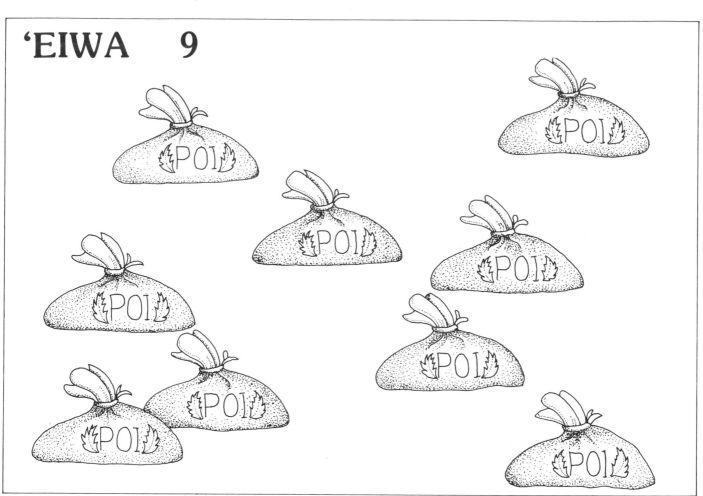

'UMI   10

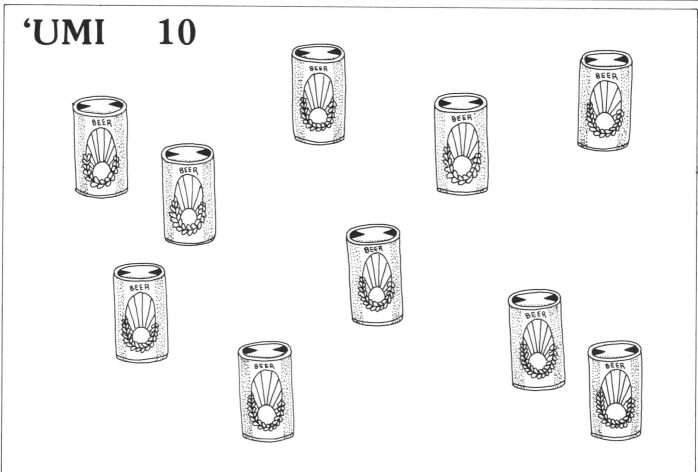

ʻUMIKŪMĀKAHI 11

ʻUMIKŪMĀLUA 12

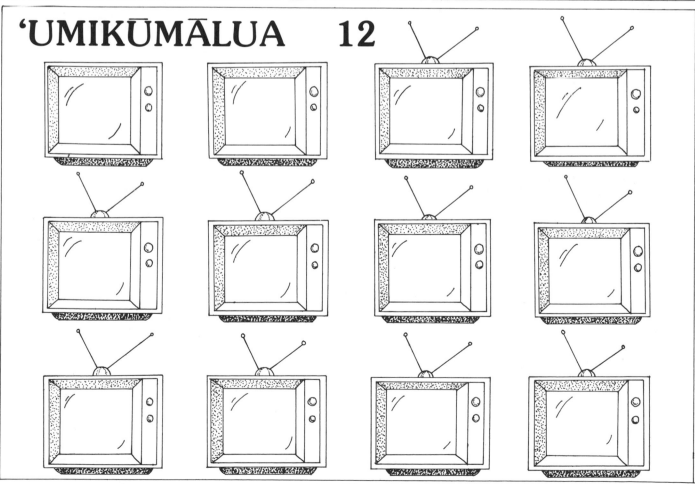

'OLE	0
IWAKĀLUA	20
KANAKOLU	30
HANELE HOʻOKAHI HANELE	100
KAUKANI HOʻOKAHI KAUKANI	1000

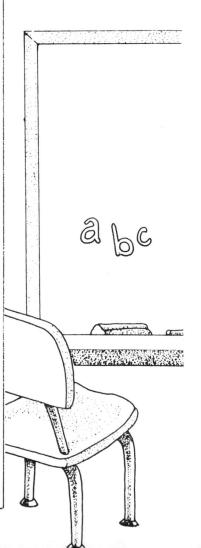

In the Classroom

kini ʻōpala	palapala ʻāina	poho
mea holoi	papaʻeleʻele	puka
nā kiʻi	peni	pukaaniani
noho	penikala	puke
pākaukau	pepa	uaki

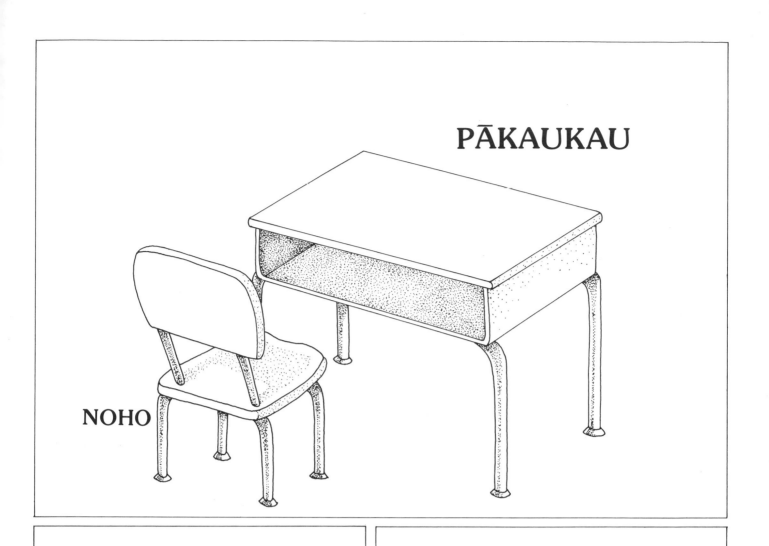

PĀKAUKAU

NOHO

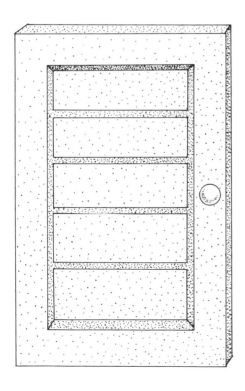

PUKA

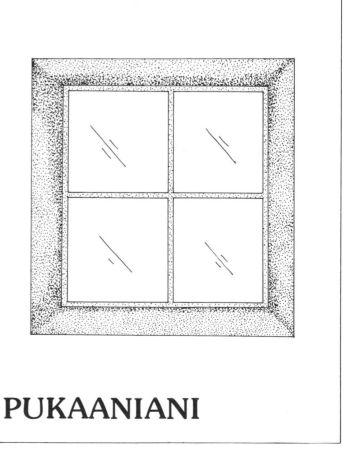

PUKAANIANI

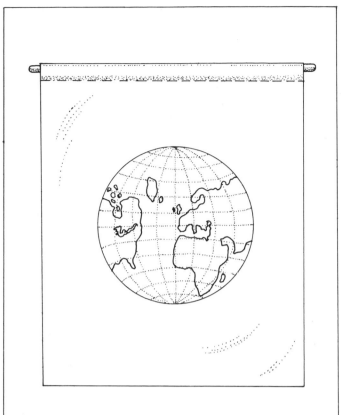

PALAPALA ʻĀINA

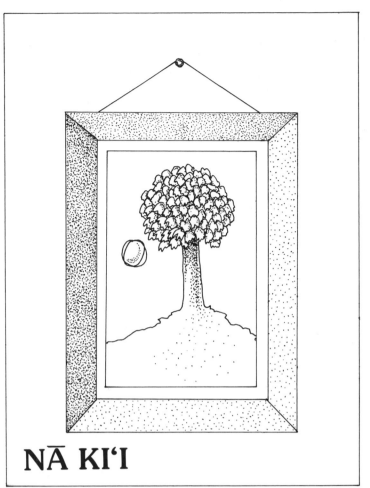

NĀ KIʻI

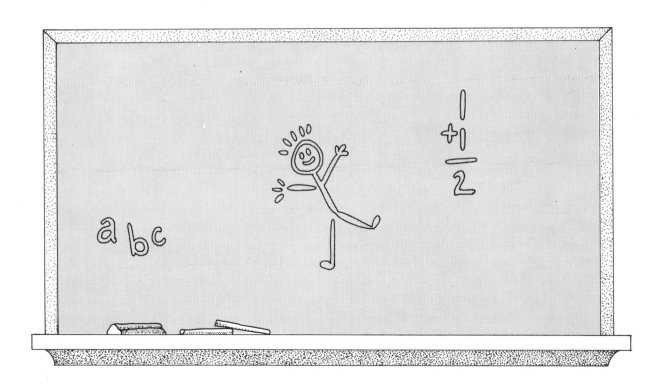

PAPAʻELEʻELE

89

PENIKALA
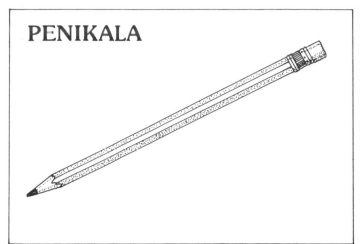

PENI
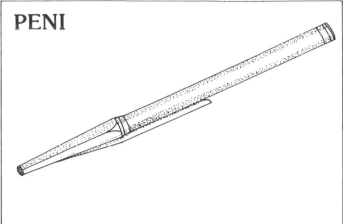

MEA HOLOI
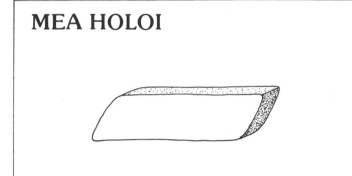

PEPA
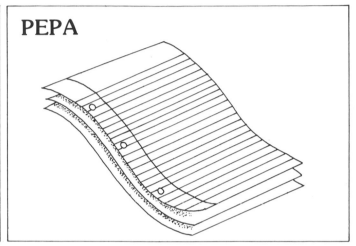

UAKI
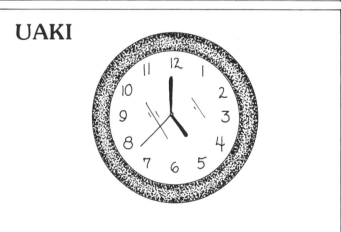

POHO
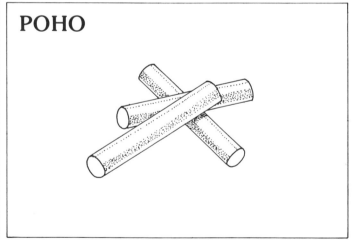

PUKE

KINI ʻŌPALA

Hawaiian Glossary

ahi — fire
ahiahi — evening
'ai — to eat; food
'a'ī — neck
ake — liver
akua — god, spirit
ala — path
'alani — orange (color)
ali'i — chief (ly), royal
aloha — love, greeting
anuanu — cold
ānuenue — rainbow
ao — cloud, daylight
'au'au — to swim, bath
'auinalā — afternoon
'auwae — chin
awakea — mid-day

'ehā — four (4)
'ehiku — seven (7)
'eiwa — nine (9)
'ekahi — one (1)
'ekolu — three (3)
'ele'ele — black
'elima — five (5)
'elua — two (2)
'eono — six (6)
'ewalu — eight (8)

ha'awi — to give
halakahiki — pineapple
hale — house
hana — to work, make or do
hanele — one hundred (100)
hau'oli — happy
he'ī — papaya
hele aku — to go (away)
hele mai — to come
helu — to count
hiamoe — to sleep
hoahānau — cousin
hoe — paddle
holo — to go, run
hōkū — star

ho'olohe — to listen
hope — after, behind; last
hou — new
hula — to dance, dance

i'a — fish
ihu — nose
'ike — to see, understand
'īlio — dog
'ino — storm, stormy
inoa — name
iwakālua — twenty (20)

kahakai — beach, seashore
kahiko — old
kahuna — expert in a profession, priest
kai — sea, sea water
kaikamahine — girl, daughter
kakahiaka — morning
kalo — taro
kama — child
kāma'a — shoe
kamaiki — baby
kanaka — person
kānaka — persons, people
kanakolu — thirty (30)
kāne — man, men
kauā (kauwā) — untouchable, outcast; slave
kaukani — one thousand (1000)
kaumaha — sad
keiki — child
keiki kāne — boy, son
ke'oke'o — white
ki'i — image, picture
kīkala — hip
kini 'ōpala — rubbish can
kino — body
kō —sugarcane
kokoke — near
kū — to stand
kua — back
kuahiwi — high hill, mountain

kuli — knee
kumulā'au — tree
kupuna — grandparent
kūpuna — grandparents
kupuna kāne — grandfather
kupuna wahine — grandmother
kupunahine — grandmother

lā — day, sun
lā'au — shrub, tree, plant
lalo — beneath, under
lau — leaf
lauoho — hair
lei — garland wreath
lele — to jump, fly
lenalena — off white, dingy yellow
lepo — dirt, dirty
li'ili'i — small
liliko'i — passion fruit
lima — hand, arm
limu — seaweed
lohe to hear
lō'ihi — long
loko — inside
lole — clothes
luna — on top, above

mahalo — praise, thanks
mahina — moon, month,
mai'a — banana
maka — eye
maka'āinana — commoner, people in general
ma kai — towards the sea
makani — wind
makua — parent
makua kāne — father
makua kāne hanauna — man in parent generation (uncle)
makuahine — mother
makuahine hanauna — woman in parent generation (aunt)
mālie — calm
malo — loin cloth

91

manamana lima — fingers

manamana wāwae — toes

manu — bird

ma uka — towards the mountains

mauna — mountain

meaʻai — food

mea holoi — eraser

melemele — yellow (golden)

moa — chicken

moana — ocean, open sea

moe — to lie down

moena — mat

momona — fat, fertile, sweet

mua — before, front, first

muʻumuʻu — loose gown

naʻau — intestines

nā kiʻi — pictures

nalu — wave, surf, full of waves

nānā — to look at

nani — beautiful

niu — coconut

noho — seat, to sit, chair

nui — big

ʻohana — family

ʻole — zero (0)

ʻōlelo — to speak

ʻōmaʻomaʻo — green

ʻono — tasty, delicious

one — sand

ʻōpū — stomach

paʻiʻai — pounded, undiluted taro

pākaukau — desk, table

palapala ʻāina — map(s)

pali — cliff

papaʻeleʻele — black board

papa heʻenalu — surfboard

pāpale — hat

pāʻū — woman's skirt, sarong

pele — volcano, eruption

peni — pen(s)

penikala — pencil

pepa — paper

pepeiao — ear

piko — navel

pō — night, darkness

pōhaku — rock, stone

poho — chalk

poi — mashed kalo, ʻuala, or ʻulu

pōkole — short

poni — purple

poʻo — head

poʻohiwi — shoulder

pua — flower

puaʻa — pig, pork

puka — hole; door, gate, opening

pukaaniani — window

puke — book

pūpū — sea shell

puʻuwai — heart

ua — rain, to rain, rainy

uaki — watch, clock

ʻuala — sweet potato

ʻūhā — thigh

uʻi — handsome

ʻulaʻula — red

uliuli — dark colors (blue, green, purple, gray) The color of the sea, sky and far off vegetation

ʻulu — breadfruit

uluna — pillow

umauma — chest

ʻumi — ten (10)

ʻumikūmākahi — eleven (11)

ʻumikūmālua — twelve (12)

ʻuʻuku — tiny

waʻa — canoe

waena — between, among

waha — mouth

wahine — woman

wāhine — women

waho — outside

wai — fresh water, stream

wailele — waterfall

wāwae — foot, leg

wela — hot

wīwī — thin, slender

English Glossary

above — luna
after — hope
afternoon — ʻauinalā
among — waena
arm — lima
aunt (women in parent generation) — makuahine hanauna

baby — kamaiki
back — kua
banana — maiʻa
bath, to bath — ʻauʻau
beach — kahakai
beautiful — nani
before — mua
behind — hope
beneath — lalo
between — waena
big — nui
bird — manu
black — ʻeleʻele
black board — papaʻeleʻele
body — kino
book — puke
breadfruit — ʻulu

calm — mālie
canoe — waʻa
chair — noho
chalk — poho
chest — umauma
chicken — moa
chief (ly) — aliʻi
child — kama, keiki
chin — ʻauwae
cliff — pali
clock — uaki
clothes — lole
cloud — ao
coconut — niu
cold — anuanu
come, to come — hele mai
commoner — makaʻāinana
count, to count — helu
cousin — hoahanau

dance — hula
daughter — kaikamahine
day — lā
delicious — ʻono
desk — pākaukau
dirt, dirty — lepo
dog — ʻīlio
door — puka

ear — pepeiao
eat, to eat — ʻai
eight (8) — ʻewalu
eleven (11) — ʻumikūmākahi
eraser — mea holoi
eruption — pele
evening — ahiahi
eye — maka

family — ʻohana
fat — momona
father — makua kāne
fingers — manamana lima
fire — ahi
first — mua
fish — iʻa
five (5) — ʻelima
flower — pua
food — meaʻai
foot — wāwae
four — ʻehā
fresh water — wai
front — mua

give, to give — haʻawi
go, to go — hele aku
god, spirit — akua
gown, loose — muʻumuʻu
grandfather — kupuna kāne
grandmother — kupuna wahine, kupunahine
grandparent — kupuna
grandparents — kūpuna
green — ʻōmaʻomaʻo

hair — lauoho

hand — lima
handsome — uʻi
happy — hauʻoli
hat — pāpale
head — poʻo
hear, to hear — lohe
heart — puʻuwai
high hill, mountain — kuahiwi
hip — kīkala
hole — puka
hot — wela
house — hale

image — kiʻi
inside — loko
intestines — naʻau

jump, to jump — lele

knee — kuli

last — hope
leaf — lau
leg — wāwae
lie down, to — moe
listen, to listen — hoʻolohe
liver — ake
loin cloth — malo
long — lōʻihi
look at, to — nānā
love, greeting — aloha

man — kāne
mat — moena
map(s) — palapala ʻāina
men — kāne
mid-day — awakea
moon — mahina
month — mahina
morning — kakahiaka
mother — makuahine
mountain — mauna, kuahiwi
mountains, toward the — ma uka
mouth — waha

name — inoa

navel — piko
near — kokoke
neck — ʻāʻī
new — hou
night (dark) — pō
nine (9) — ʻeiwa
nose — ihu

ocean, open sea — moana
old — kahiko
on top — luna
one (1) — ʻekahi
one hundred (100) — hanele
one thousand (1000) — kaukani
opening — puka
orange — ʻalani
outcast — kauā (kauwā)
outside — waho

paddle — hoe
papaya — hēʻī
paper — pepa
passion fruit — lilikoʻi
parent — makua
parents — mākua
path — ala
pen — peni
pencil — penikala
person — kanaka
persons, people — kānaka
picture — kiʻi
pictures — nā kiʻi
pig — puaʻa
pillow — uluna
pineapple — halakahiki
praise — mahalo
priest — kahuna
purple — poni

rain, rainy — ua

rainbow — ānuenue
red — ʻulaʻula
rock — pōhaku
royal — aliʻi
rubbish can — kini ʻōpala
run, to run — holo

sad — kaumaha
sand — one
sea, sea water — kai
sea shell — pūpū
sea, toward the — ma kai
seashore — kahakai
seat — noho
seaweed — limu
see, to know — ʻike
seven — ʻehiku
shoe — kāmaʻa
short — pōkole
shoulder — poʻohiwi
shrub — lāʻau
sit, to sit — noho
six (6) — ʻeono
skirt, sarong — pāʻū
slave — kauā (kauwā)
sleep, to sleep — hiamoe
slender — wīwī
small — liʻiliʻi
son — keiki kāne
speak, to speak — ʻōlelo
stand, to stand — kū
star — hōkū
stomach — ʻōpū
stone — pōhaku
storm, stormy — ʻino
sugar cane — kō
sun — lā
surf — nalu

surfboard — papa heʻenalu
swim, to swim — ʻauʻau

table — pākaukau
taro — kalo
taro, undiluted pounded — paʻiʻai
ten — ʻumi
thanks — mahalo
thigh — ʻūhā
thin — wīwī
thirty — kanakolu
three (3) — ʻekolu
tiny — ʻuʻuku
toes — manamana wāwae
tree — kumulāʻau, lāʻau
twelve (12) — ʻumikūmālua
twenty (20) — iwakālua
two (2) — ʻelua

uncle (man in parent generation)
   — makua kāne hanauna
under — lalo

volcano — pele

watch (clock) — uaki
water, fresh — wai
water, salt or sea — kai
waterfall — wailele
wave — nalu
white — keʻokeʻo
wind — makani
window — pukaaniani
woman — wahine
women — wāhine
work, to work — hana

yellow (golden) — melemele

zero (0) — ʻole

PRONUNCIATION GUIDE
OR HOW TO SAY HAWAIIAN WORDS

Hawaiian consonants are *h, k, l, m, n, p,* and *w.* They are said the same as they are in English. Sometimes people say *w* differently. After *i* and *e* the *w* usually sounds like *v,* (iwa-a large sea bird, Ewa-a town on Oʻahu). After *u* and *o* it usually sounds like *w,* (kauwā-an outcast, wohi-a kind of high chief). After *a* or at the beginning of a word or syllable it may sound like either *w* or *v,* (Hawaiʻi or Haw̌aiʻi).

Hawaiian words have many vowels. Every word or syllable ends in a vowel. The vowel sounds are:

WHEN STRESSED	WHEN NOT STRESSED
a, a—like *a* in *was:* olonā	a—like *a* in *was:* aliʻi
e—like *e* in *bet:* menehune	e—like *e* in *bet:* Pele
ē—like a in *baby:* nēnē	i—like *e* in *he:* kiʻi
i, ī—like *e* in *he:* mōʻī	o—like *o* in *go:* milo
o, ō—like *o* in *go:* kōkō	u—like *oo* in *moon:* pahu
u, ū—like *oo* in *moon:* pāʻū	

Hawaiian words are usually stressed on the next to the last syllable unless there is a single line over a vowel (ā). This is called a macron or kahakō. It shows that the vowel should be said with stress or longer and stronger. Olonā is the name of a Hawaiian plant. The *ā* is said longer and stronger. Some words have two or more of these marks. A pāʻū is a woman's skirt. Both vowels are said with stress.

Sometimes two vowels go together. These are called diphthongs. The vowel sounds are the same and are rolled together as you say them with the first one being stronger. Hawaiian diphthongs are: *ei, eu, oi, ou, ai, ao, au.*

In some Hawaiian words you will see a little mark like an apostrophe (ʻ). It marks a glottal stop. In Hawaiian this mark is called an ʻuʻina or ʻokina. It shows that there is a break in the word, like saying the English *oh-oh.*